THE LAFAYETTE WHITE CROSS PROTEST MEMORIAL

MARQUIS PUBLISHING
LARKSPUR, CALIFORNIA

Version 2.1

Published by Marquis Publishing
Larkspur, California

Vickers, Marques, 1957

The Lafayette White Cross Protest Memorial

To The Brave Combatants Whose Only Voice Remains From The Survivors Back Home. My Daughters Charline and Caroline.

TABLE OF CONTENTS

Preface

The five-year California drought has finally succumbed to the traditional and belated rains of winter. If only the elimination of warfare and its accompanying casualties were as simplistic. When I began this photo project in mid-2014, there were already 6809 deaths registered on the memorial sign.

For eight years previously, I had become vaguely familiar with this significant hillside, periodically passing and viewing the escalating count. One day hopefully we may not require this reminder.

That day is not today. The protest against inhumanity and global violence should constantly remain in the forefront of our thoughts. Otherwise the remembrance of those who sacrificed their lives on our behalf is without value.

Peace is a complicated process but aggression is always against everyone's best interests.

Conflict and Remembrance (2017)

Over two and a half years have elapsed since I originally photographed the Lafayette Cross Memorial. Over two hundred additional military casualties have been added to the prominently posted tally board. The total now exceeds 7,000. There are not enough crosses for each casualty. There is insufficient land to contain the accumulated sorrow.

Each cross represents a silent cry of loss for the bereaved.

Armed conflict has not ceased globally, but the pace of conventional battlefield deaths has slowed. The nature of warfare has shifted.

Civilian casualties through urban terrorist actions have emerged as flash points for armed conflict. Each widely media scrutinized aggression advances the exposure and terror of these reputed causes and soldiers without uniforms.

On a global scale, the threat of nuclear Armageddon has not receded based on recent irresponsible posturing by certain world leaders. The rampant employment of nuclear weaponry remains a legitimate concern. Killing efficiency has heightened with technology. A fired exchange of nuclear arms will accelerate the scale of casualties and create an unwinnable scenario for participating parties.

Despite our enormous advances in communication technology, we still have not learned how to properly dialogue, understand each other and suspend the menace of violence.

Pacifism remains unfashionable and confused with weakness. Protest against the absurdity and insanity of war, however, is never irrelevant. The peace movement sometimes seems impractical when foreign aggressive militaries and fanatic causes are anxious to replace any vacuum created by an American withdrawal. The world remains suspended in standoff and civilization is held hostage.

A renew rhetoric of nationalism creates a fragile future. Separatism and isolation launched the United States into two global wars during the twentieth century. What will be our fate and future in the twenty-first century?

Humanity has still not learned to live together and propaganda exploits that abyss. One sad day, should the Lafayette Cross Memorial remain, the posted figure may surpass five digits. We are already nearly three-quarters there since its inception ten years ago.

The future victims fated to join their fallen brethren and sisters will pay the ultimate tariff for the turbulence and hostilities. The elected leaders and supreme commanders that will lead them to their fate will remain removed and secure from physical harm.

This paradox is the irony of a soldier's legacy and a continuing tragedy we have never learned to eradicate.

The Lafayette White Cross Memorial Hillside

Why are we visually drawn towards the simplest expressions of remembrance? The makeshift roadside testimonials, liberally piled flower arrangements and hand scrawled cardboard signs reveal raw and poignant pain derived from loss.

Collective loss becomes challenging to express. Within the United States, our civic centers, public parks and countryside's are littered with bronze casted memorials. Their intention is remembrance yet over time their appearance may become taken for granted and easily ignored. Solemn ceremonies and pageantry periodically remind us of their significance even when their visual impact has long ago dimmed.

The Lafayette, California Hillside Cross Memorial is stark, profound and impressive, although not particularly aesthetic. The impact of over 4000 bleached crosses is stirring. Its immediate force and power are relevant based on its history and the ongoing preservation by dedicated volunteers.

Such a memorial transcends any creator's original intent. In November of 2006, the message was a solemn and ultimately futile protest against American involvement in the Iraq War. Support for the Memorial was initially unpopular by many. Protest and dissension against American foreign policy was unwelcomed amidst an American casualty rate escalating daily in a military struggle that had clearly lost its bearings.

The American military had easily routed the Iraqi army and then President Saddam Hussein in actual armed conflict within one brief month during 2003. Then, the true controversy and casualties began during the occupation phase over the subsequent eight years. Today most individuals have come to regard the Cross Memorial as a reminder that war, in whatever context, erases innocence and exacts a demanding outlay from our nation's youth.

As the casualty totals have since encompassed the Afghanistan conflict and our military death toll has surpassed 6800 victims, the hillside has become dwarfed by the number of implanted crosses. In August of 2011, organizers ceased adding crosses. The numerical accuracy became secondary to the symbolic gesture. Death pays no attention to order and straightly formational columns. The crosses are situated erratically but the effect remains profound. A 32-square-foot sign in the midst tallies a running total of the death count since 2003 and is updated weekly.

The inclined property overlooks one of Contra Costa County's freeway arteries and the Lafayette BART transit station. The Clark family owns the land. Louise Clark, now diseased originally sanctioned the project coordinated by Jeffrey Heaton, a longtime regional anti-war protestor. The fate of the monument today remains unclear and discussions regarding its future continue between the heirs, civic organizations and local officials.

Nature has contributed its own destructive patina and many of the crosses stagger in states of deterioration. These realities fade into insignificance when one simply surveys the visual impression from a distance. One day too the Memorial's iconic authority may fade into redundancy. One day it may be replaced by a tidier, more concentrated sculptural theme. One day, the crosses may be simply uprooted.

For now its command and relevance remain in the immediate tense.

The impulsively constructed Memorial was controversial from its inception. Vocal outrage and staged protests criticized both its purpose and existence. Certain outspoken war veterans found the public display insulting and derogatory to those soldiers who'd lost their lives in combat. Vandals defiantly defaced and stole crosses. City officials required cross organizers to shrink the original sign displaying the number of troops killed in Iraq.

The remembrance of war is divisive. The Memorial endured. The casualty figures have slowed to a trickle. America's involvement in Iraq and Afghanistan has subsided but global military conflict and response remain an unrelenting and lucrative enterprise.

The Crosses of Lafayette are probably the largest memorial of its kind in post 9/11 and likely the most personal. Traditional white crosses are accompanied by some bearing the Star of David, Islamic crescents, Buddhist prayer wheels and other religious symbolism. Several feature attached photographs, writings and other personal mementos.

Each personalized cross conveys a narrative about loss and how we remember those fighting and dying so far away from their home.

Visual Artist, Writer and Photographer Marques Vickers is a California native presently living in the San Francisco Bay Area and Seattle, Washington regions.

He was born in 1957 and raised in Vallejo, California. He is a 1979 Business Administration graduate from Azusa Pacific University in the Los Angeles area. Following graduation, he became the Public Relations and ultimately Executive Director of the Burbank Chamber of Commerce between 1979-84. He subsequently became the Vice President of Sales for AsTRA Tours and Travel in Westwood between 1984-86.

Following a one-year residence in Dijon, France where he studied at the University of Bourgogne, he began Marquis Enterprises in 1987. His company operations have included sports apparel exporting, travel and tour operations, wine brokering, publishing, rare book and collectibles reselling. He has established numerous e-commerce, barter exchange and art websites including MarquesV.com, ArtsInAmerica.com, InsiderSeriesBooks.com, DiscountVintages.com and WineScalper.com.

Between 1988-2005, he was a full-time Catholic high school instructor in his hometown of Vallejo, California.

Between 2005-2009, he relocated to the Languedoc region of southern France. He concentrated on his painting and sculptural work while restoring two 19th century stone village residences. His figurative painting, photography and sculptural works have been sold and exhibited internationally since 1986. Between 2008-2011, he was a part-time instructor in the Benicia Unified School district. He re-established his Pacific Coast residence in 2009 and has focused his creative productivity on writing and photography.

His published works span a diverse variety of subjects including true crime, international travel, California wines, architecture, history, Southern France, Pacific Coast attractions, auctions, fine art marketing, poetry, fiction and photojournalism.

He has two daughters, Charline and Caroline who presently reside in Europe.

BOOKS:
Marketing and Buying Fine Art Online, Allworth Press, New York NY (2005)
Making Auction Pay, Marquis Publications, Vallejo CA. (2014)
Unicorns and Dark Chocolate: Eros, Aphrodesia and Existence, Marquis Publications, Vallejo CA (2014)
Amour, Wine and Real Estate, Marquis Publications, Vallejo CA (2014)
Flamenco Jondo: The Paintings of Marques Vickers, Marquis Publications, Vallejo CA (2014)
The Ultimate Guide to Selling Art Online, Marquis Publications, Vallejo CA (2014)
The Lafayette White Cross Memorial, Marquis Publications, Vallejo CA (2014)

2014 Napa Valley Earthquake, Marquis Publications, Vallejo CA (2014)

Fish Head Beach: The Silent and Senseless Murders of Lindsay Cutshall and Jason Allen, Marquis Publications, Vallejo CA (2014)

Muse One: Pantera Linda, Marquis Publications, Vallejo CA (2014)

Nature As Art: One, Marquis Publications, Vallejo CA (2014)

Springtime in New England, Marquis Publications, Vallejo CA (2014)

San Antonio Riverwalk, Marquis Publications, Vallejo CA (2014)

Ruined Castles and Phantom Memories, Marquis Publications, Vallejo CA (2014)

Sand and Water: Desert and Seascapes, Marquis Publications, Vallejo CA (2014)

Napa Rebuilds: Two Months Following Their Devastating Earthquake, Marquis Publications, Vallejo CA (2014)

The 2014 Napa Valley Wine Harvest, Marquis Publications, Vallejo CA (2014)

The Topography of Evil: Notorious Northern California Murder Sites, Marquis Publications, Vallejo CA (2015)

The Disappearing Women, Marquis Publications, Morro Beach CA (2015)

Five Month of Renovation After the 2014 Napa Earthquake, Marquis Publications, Morro Bay CA (2015)

100 Famous Phobias and Obsessions: An Entertaining Portrayal of Anxiety, Fears and Insecurity As Artwork, Marquis Publications, Morro Bay CA (2015)

Visions of Neo-Urbania: The Reinvention of Contemporary Metropolitan Vertical Living and Commerce, Marquis Publications, Tacoma WA (2015)

Nature As Art Two: Photography and Abstract Paintings of Marques Vickers, Marquis Publications, Tacoma WA (2015)

Morro Rock: Veiled Bridge of the Nine Sisters, Marquis Publications, Tacoma WA (2015)

Eternal Spring Street: Los Angeles' Architectural Reincarnation, Marquis Publications, Tacoma WA (2015)

The Reflective Powers of Water As Visual Alchemy, Marquis Publications, Tacoma WA (2015)

Jimi Hendrix, Bruce and Brandon Lee and the Lakeview Cemetery Seattle: Entombing Our Icons, Marquis Publications, Renton WA (2015)

The Artistic Properties of Reflective Glass, Marquis Publications, Renton WA (2015)

The Glass Curtain Architecture of Bellevue, Washington, Marquis Publications, Renton WA (2015)

Murder in California: Notorious California Murder Sites, Marquis Publications, Renton WA (2015)

Coffee Anarchists of the World Unite: The Italian Roasted Elixirs of Tacoma, Washington, Marquis Publications, Renton WA (2015)

The Abandoned Western Cascade Mountain Railroad Tunnels and 1910 Wellington Avalanche, Marquis Publications, Renton WA (2015)

The 2014 Napa Earthquake and Anniversary Aftermath: A Fourteenth Month Retrospective Into Historical Downtown Napa, Marquis Publications, Concord CA (2015)

Murder in Washington: The Topography of Evil, Marquis Publications, Larkspur CA (2016)

The Architectural Elevation of Technology: A Photo Survey of 75 Silicon Valley Headquarters, Marquis Publishing, Edmonds, WA (2016)

Reinventing Broadway Street: Los Angeles Architectural Reincarnation, Marquis Publishing, Edmonds, WA (2016)

So You Think You Know California Wine? (2016) The Grape Divide: Demystifying the Economics of Wine, Marquis Publishing, Edmonds, WA (2016)

Unseen Marin: The Waterways of Marin County, California, Marquis Publications, Edmonds, WA (2016)

Tulip Universe, Marquis Publications, Edmonds, WA (2016)

Unseen Marin: The Waterways of Mill Valley, Marquis Publications, Edmonds, WA (2016)

Unseen Marin: The Waterways of Central Marin County, Marquis Publications, Edmonds, WA (2016)

Unseen Marin: The Waterways of San Rafael and Fairfax, Marquis Publications, Edmonds, WA (2016)

When Letters Still Mattered: An Autobiography Based on Correspondence, Marquis Publications, Edmonds, WA (2016)

Lake Union: The Public Face of Prosperity, The Vertical Seattle Series, Marquis Publications, Edmonds, WA (2016)

101 Surrealistic Phobias and Obsessions, Marquis Publications, Edmonds, WA (2016)

So You Think You Know Washington State Wines? (2016-17) *Demystifying the Economics of Wine*, Marquis Publishing, Edmonds, WA (2016)

Teaching With One Eye Shut, Volume One, Marquis Publications, Edmonds, WA (2016)

Leaving Teaching With Both Eyes Open, Volume Two, Marquis Publications, Edmonds, WA (2016)

Vertical Bellevue: Architecture Above A Boomburb Skyline, Marquis Publications, Edmonds, WA (2016)

Vladimir Putin and Dresden, Germany: The Genesis of Myth Making, Marquis Publications, Frankfurt Am Main, Germany (2016)

The Berlin Wall: Over 25 Years After the Fall, Marquis Publications, Frankfurt Am Main, Germany (2016)

102 Satirical Photographic Ironies: Subtle to Subversive, Marquis Publications, Frankfurt Am Main, Germany (2016)

16-Hour Oregon Coast Road Trip: A Photographic Narrative, Marquis Publications, Larkspur, CA (2016)

Architect John D. Parkinson: Eternally Elevating the Los Angeles Skyline, Marquis Publications, Larkspur, CA (2017)

www.ingramcontent.com/pod-product-compliance
Lightning Source LLC
Chambersburg PA
CBHW062048280526
45788CB00003B/1147